Love to Sew
Little Bags & Purses

WITHDRAWN
1 8 MAY 2024
CLARA

D1347316

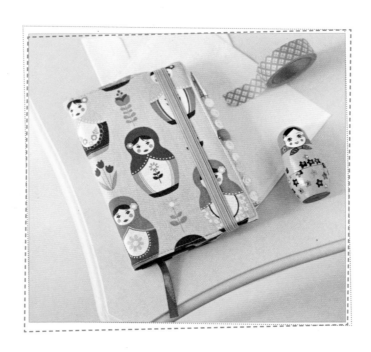

Love to Sew

Little Bags & Purses

Saskia Abel

Search Press

First published in Great Britain 2015 by Search Press Limited
Wellwood, North Farm Road, Tunbridge Wells, Kent TN2 3DR

Original German edition published as *Kleine Taschen*

Copyright © 2014 Christophorus Verlag GmbH,
Freiburg/Germany

Text copyright © Saskia Abel 2014

English translation by Burravoe Translation Services

All rights reserved. No part of this book, text, photographs or
illustrations may be reproduced or transmitted in any form
or by any means by print, photoprint, microfilm, microfiche,
photocopier, internet or in any way known or as yet unknown,
or stored in a retrieval system, without written permission
obtained beforehand from Search Press.

ISBN: 978-1-78221-223-2

Designs: Saskia Abel
Technical drawings: Claudia Schmidt
Photography: Uli Glasemann
Styling: Elke Reith

The publishers and author can accept no responsibility for
any consequences arising from the information, advice or
instructions given in this publication.

Printed in China

Glasses Case, page 16

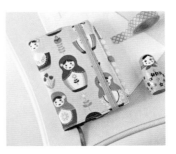

Book Cover, page 18

Phone bag, page 25

Notebook Cover, page 28

Tablet Case, page 36

Phone Cover, page 38

Key Case, page 44

Tablet Cover, page 47

Wallet, page 20

Purse, page 31

Tissue Case, page 40

Make-up Bag, page 50

Contents

Bag Organiser, page 23

Pencil Case, page 34

Fabric Key Ring, page 42

Card Carrier, page 53

Introduction

We all know it – the chaos that reigns when we're trying to find our house or car keys in the depths of a cluttered handbag. The idea behind this book was to design lots of helpful little bags to make life easier – and perhaps a bit more colourful too!

In addition to essential items such as a key ring and phone cover, this book contains a practical bag organiser, a lovely make-up bag, a card carrier and a tablet cover – as well as lots of other helpers.

Some of the items are easier to make than others, and not only are they all suitable for your own bag, but they also make perfect birthday or Christmas presents for friends, family members or someone you work with. In any case, these handmade wonders are bound to create a lasting impression.

I hope you enjoy making them, and perhaps even creating your own ideas. With any luck, these little bags and purses will be the perfect solution for solving that messy handbag problem.

Happy sewing,

Saskia Abel

The projects are graded according to how easy they are:

Quick and easy ♡
Requires a little practice ♡ ♡
More challenging ♡ ♡ ♡

Materials & tools

These little bags and purses are all fairly straightforward to sew so you will only require the most basic of sewing materials to get started. These items are not listed separately in the project instructions as it is assumed that you will have these to hand:

Sewing machine: you'll need a reliable sewing machine with a straight stitch and some embroidery stitches for decoration.

Matching threads: make sure you have a wide variety of sewing and embroidery threads at your disposal, as well as cotton yarns for embellishing your projects.

Steam iron: essential when working with fabric.

Fabrics: you will need a good stash of cotton or polyester fabrics in a variety of patterns.

Hand-sewing needles: make sure you have a good selection of needles in a range of sizes that will suit different thicknesses of fabric and thread.

Pattern paper: this will be useful for transferring the templates from the back of the book to fabric.

Water-soluble pen and tailor's chalk: essential for marking pattern outlines and seams on your fabric.

Scissors: a sharp pair of fabric scissors is essential. You may also find that a good pair of pinking shears will come in handy to give a decorative edge to your fabrics and to stop them from fraying. You will also require a small pair of embroidery scissors for the finer details.

Pins: you will need a good selection of pins to hold your fabrics in place. A magnetic pin holder is a helpful tool for holding all your pins – or, failing that, a pincushion.

Tape measure: make sure you have one of these to accurately measure the fabrics for each project.

Seam ripper: it is often useful to have a seam ripper on hand for any sewing mistakes, or to salvage fabric from old clothes.

Rotary cutter or carpet knife: a useful tool for cutting fabric.

Cutting mat: this is useful to protect your worksurface when cutting.

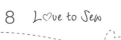

Sewing basics

Tension

Adjust the tension on your sewing machine to suit the particular fabric as otherwise you could end up with loops in the upper or lower thread. Ideally, always try it out on a test piece first.

Straight stitch

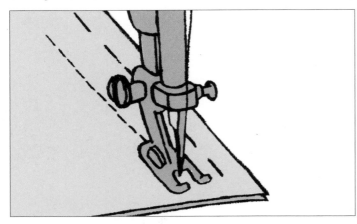

This is the basic utility stitch on a sewing machine. It might also be called lockstitch. You can adjust the stitch length to suit your purposes. The longer the stitch is, the looser the seam will be.

Tacking and pinning

Before sewing, always secure the pieces of fabric by tacking a seam by hand or pinning them. This will prevent the pieces of fabric from sliding and creases from forming when you sew them together.

The run of the thread

Every material is made up of warp threads (lengthways) and weft threads (crossways). The run of the thread corresponds to the direction of the warp threads, and goes parallel to the fabric selvedge. The fabric should always be cut in the run of the thread to prevent the sewn item from distorting.

Seam allowance

The seam allowance is the gap that is kept before the cut edge when sewing. It prevents the fabric from tearing. With the designs shown here, the seam allowance is generally 0.5cm (¼in) to 0.7cm (½in). The width of the seam allowance is given under "Cutting out" in the project instructions.

Right and wrong side of the fabric

Every piece of fabric has a right and a wrong side. The right side is the side that we see, i.e. the outside of the fabric. This is easy to identify on printed fabrics as it is the side where the pattern is clearer. So when the instructions tell you to "place the pieces of fabric with the right sides facing", this means that the right sides (the sides that we normally see) should be together on the inside, and the wrong sides (that we don't normally see) are on the outside. And if the instructions say "wrong sides facing" then the right sides should be on the outside and the wrong sides on the inside.

Fabric fold

Folding a piece of fabric in half creates a folded edge that is called the fold of the fabric or fold line. On a pattern piece, the fold is usually the middle of the cut-out item. In this book, the fold is shown as a broken line. This edge is placed exactly on the fabric fold without a seam allowance when cutting out.

Zigzag stitch

Zigzag stitch is used to neaten cut edges. The stitch length and width can be adjusted. A very tight zigzag stitch can also be used to sew pieces of fabric on without having to fold the edges under to prevent fraying.

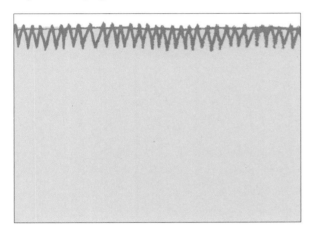

Basic techniques

Neat seams

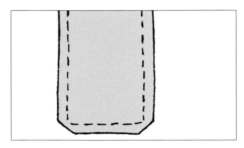

The right sides of the fabric are placed together with the raw edges flush with each other. The items are then sewn together apart from a turning opening. Trim the seam allowances at an angle at the corners so they lie better and look neater after turning.

Neat curves

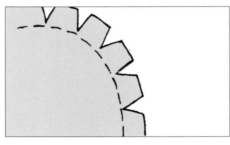

For rounded items, cut the seam allowances, as shown, to approximately 1mm (¹⁄₁₆in) before the stitch, with small gaps between the individual cuts, before turning the item right side out. The rounded section will then look neatly rounded after turning, because any pieces of excess fabric can slide over each other.

Stitch the ends of the base

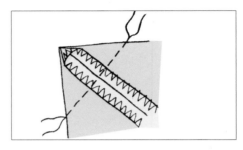

Align the side and base seams of the corner over each other. This creates a triangle with the seams in the middle. Sew the triangle crosswise to the seam. This area is already omitted in the pattern pieces, so all you have to do is sew the base opening.

Using bias binding

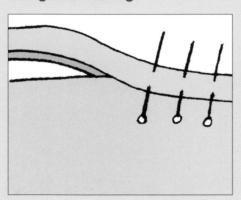

1 Fold pre-folded bias binding in half lengthwise with the wrong sides facing, and iron a fold down the middle. Push the fabric edge into the fold of the bias binding and pin to secure.

2 The bias binding should be straight, with the width the same all along the front and back pieces. Then sew the bias binding close to the inner folded edge.

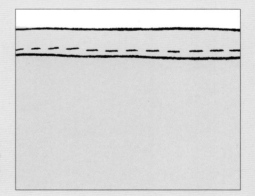

Sewing piping

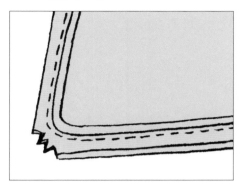

1 Tack the piping to the right side of the fabric, along the marked sewing line. The thick cord of the piping will be folded on the inside of the piece of sewing. Tack the second piece of fabric to the first with the right sides together. Sew all around leaving a turning opening close to the cord inside the piping.

2 Turn the item right side out. The piping will now be on the inside, running along the seam.

Inserting a zip

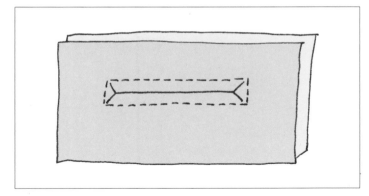
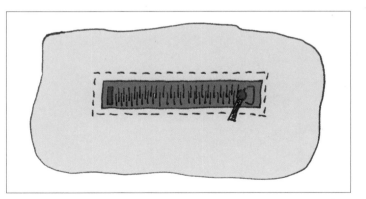

1 Place the fabric pieces together with the right sides facing. Draw a square 1cm (½in) wide and the length of the zip. Tack this line. Cut diagonally into the square between the tacking lines and in the corners

2 Draw the lining to the inside through the cut. Iron the edges. Place the zip on the middle of the back under the triangle and sew in small stitches.

Projects

Choose from this wonderful range of pretty and useful bags and purses to sew. You can use the fabrics listed in the materials section of each project, or your own choice of patterns.

The templates you need are all provided at the end of the book.

Materials

- A: fabric in a tulip pattern (front/back), 15 x 50cm (6 x 19¾in)
- B: striped fabric (lining), 15 x 50cm (6 x 19¾in)
- C: medium iron-on volume fleece, 15 x 50cm (6 x 19¾in)
- 1 heart shaped eyeglass or metal purse frame, 5 x 17cm (2 x 6¾in)
- white sewing thread
- textile adhesive
- pliers and a piece of felt or fabric

Cutting out

Pattern includes 0.5cm (¼in) seam allowance
- A: 2 pieces of pattern 1
- B: 2 pieces of pattern 1
- C: 2 pieces of pattern 1

Glasses Case

Size: 8 x 19cm (3¼ x 7½in)   Pattern piece: 1 on page 56
Level of difficulty: ♡ ♡

How to do it

1 Iron the wrong sides of the two pieces of fabric A onto the two pieces of volume fleece C. Place the two pieces of fabric A together with the right sides facing and sew the bottom edge between the marks * (see pattern). Sew together the fabric pieces leaving a turning opening of 8cm (3¼in) at the bottom.

2 Place fabrics A inside fabric B with the right sides facing. Align the top edges neatly, and sew together on all sides (but not the top edges).

3 Turn the case right side out. Iron well along the top edges, and edge stitch as close to the edge as you can.

4 Drip textile adhesive into the back of the frame. Be careful not to use too much or it will leak out and leave a mess on the fabric. Push the back of the case into the frame, starting in the middle. Use a fork or something similarly flat and blunt to help.

5 Use pliers to squeeze the two bottom ends of the frame onto the fabric. Put a piece of felt or fabric between the pliers and the metal so you don't scratch the frame. Don't squeeze too hard as you will mark the metal. Check to make sure that fabrics A and B are both well positioned in the frame.

6 Repeat for the front. Leave the case open for about 24 hours. Use a little water and a piece of fabric to rub off any leftover adhesive on the frame. You will not be able to do this later on.

Note

Make sure that the seam allowance is such that you can fit the case inside the metal frame.

Book Cover

Size: 15 x 10cm (6 x 4in) Level of difficulty: ♡ ♡

Materials

- A: fabric in a matryoshka pattern (front/back), 18 x 35cm (7 x 13¾in)
- B: fabric in a dusky pink (lining), 18 x 35cm (7 x 13¾in)
- green elastic, 1cm (½in) wide and approximately 37cm (14½in) long
- pins
- pink sewing thread

Cutting out

Dimensions include 0.5cm (¼in) seam allowance

- A: 1 rectangle measuring 15 x 30cm (6 x 11¾in)
- B: 1 rectangle measuring 15 x 30cm (6 x 11¾in)

How to do it

1 Lie fabric A down, right side up; the short edges are the sides. Cut a piece of elastic measuring about 18.5cm (7¼in) and sew to the top and bottom edges 7.5cm (3in) from the left edge. The elastic should protrude beyond the edge by about 1cm (½in).

2 Cut a piece of elastic measuring 15cm (6in) for the pen holder, and fold in half. Pin to the left side edge of fabric A in the middle on the outer side of the fabric. The elastic loop should point inwards beyond the planned folded edge by about 0.5cm (¼in). Sew the folded piece of elastic in place leaving a gap of 1.5cm (¾in) – this is where the pen will go.

3 With the right sides facing, pin the short seams of fabrics A and B neatly together and sew all round, leaving a turning opening of about 5cm (2in) at the bottom. Turn the cover right side out. Carefully push out the corners, and iron. Turn the seam allowances of the turning opening to the inside and pin.

4 Turn the fold on the left side edge over by 4.75cm (1¾in) and the same on the right, and pin. Check to make sure the book will fit. There should be a little give along the side edges. Then edge stitch along all sides, including the turning opening. Sew the folded sections three times. Make sure that the elastic closure is on the back, and take care not to sew over the pen holder.

Note

These dimensions will fit an A6 notepad 18mm (about ¾in) wide. If your notepad is different, adjust the measurements accordingly. Place the book on the fabric and fold over. The fabric fold should measure 5cm (2in) + a total of 1cm (½in) seam allowance and 0.5cm (¼in) for sewing.

Materials

- A: fabric in a penguin pattern (flap), 12 x 25cm (4¾ x 9¾in)
- B: black fabric with white dots (zip compartment/back), 50 x 20cm (19¾ x 7¾in)
- C: back fabric with white flowers (note compartment), 20 x 25cm (7¾ x 9¾in)
- D: black fabric (bag/lining), 40 x 25cm (15¾ x 9¾in)
- E: yellow fabric with white dots (lining zip compartment), 25 x 30cm (9¾ x 11¾in)
- F: thick, fluffy volume fleece, 30 x 25cm (11¾ x 9¾in)
- G: lightweight iron-on interfacing, 11 x 25cm (4¼ x 9¾in)
- 1 black zip, 15cm (6in)
- 1 loop, 5mm (¼in) diameter
- green elastic cord, 2mm (⅛in) diameter, 45cm (17¾in)
- green piping with white dots, 40cm (15¾in)
- wax cloth, felt or similar, 4 x 4cm (1½ x 1½in)
- sewing thread in black and white
- pins

Cutting out

Dimensions and patterns include 0.5cm (¼in) seam allowance.

- A: 1 piece of pattern 4a
- B: 1 each of patterns 4a and 4b, 1 rectangle d of 9.5 x 23cm (3¾ x 9in), front of note compartment, 1 rectangle e of 11.5 x 23cm (4½ x 9in), back of note compartment
- C: 1 piece of pattern 4c
- D: 3 pieces of pattern 4b
- E: 1 rectangle of 9.5 x 23cm (3¾ x 9in), 1 rectangle e of 11.5 x 23cm (4½ x 9in)
- F: 2 pieces of pattern 4b
- G: 1 piece of pattern 4a

Wallet

Size: 10 x 18cm (4 x 7in) • **Pattern pieces:** 4a–c on pages 58–59
Level of difficulty: ♡ ♡ ♡

How to do it

1 Iron interfacing G onto the back of fabric A. Lay the piping flush with the rounded edge on the right side of fabric A and sew into place. Check to establish which position the sewing foot and needle need to be in so that only the piping can be seen later. Place fabric B/4a on fabric A with the right sides facing and sew along the outer edge. Leave the top edge open. Turn right side out, iron and edge stitch.

2 For the zip compartment, position fabric B/d with the right side up and put the zip flush and in the middle of the top edge with the right sides facing (so the underside of the zip should be at the top with the zip pull on the left); there should be some fabric left at the sides. Place fabric E/d on fabric B/d neatly and with the right sides facing, and pin the zip. Sew the two layers and zip securely using the zip foot of your sewing machine. Iron the fabric pieces well, and edge stitch along the side of the zip, working close to the edge.

3 With the right sides facing, pin fabric B/e to the other side of the zip. With the right sides facing, place fabric E/e onto fabric E that has already been sewn into place, then pin to fabric B/e and the zip, and sew securely. Turn the pieces right side out. Iron and sew the second edge. Set aside.

4 Sew the zip compartment (B) to the note compartment (C/4c). Iron the zip compartment so that 0.5cm (¼in) of the fabric protrudes beyond the top of the zip. Position the zip compartment at a distance of 1cm (½in) from the top of the note compartment. Make sure that the ends of the zip are flush with the sides of the note compartment. Pin, turn and trim the zip compartment to the shape of the note compartment.

5 Now prepare the top edge for the credit card slot. Sew the top edge of the zip compartment to the inside of the note compartment about 3cm (1¼in) from the sides. Put your credit card in the slot. Raise the front of the zip compartment (B/E) and mark the bottom edge of the card on the back of the zip compartment (E/B) with a pin. On fabrics E and B of the back, sew a seam the length of the credit card. Sew the compartments to fabric D/4b (with F) with the bottom edges flush.

6 Place the second fabric D/4b on the finished bag with the right sides facing and sew along the top edge. Open out the fabrics and edge stitch along the top edge of the bag.

7 With the right sides facing, place the bag flap flush in the middle of fabric B/4b (with F), and place the remaining fabric D/4b on top, again with the right sides facing. Pin, then sew all the layers together. Open out the fabrics so that the flap and lining are on the right and the back of the bag is on the left. Edge stitch along the top of the back piece.

8 Pin the front and back together with the right sides facing, making sure that all the corners line up exactly. Pin the lining together down the side edges and along the bottom.

9 Start to sew up the bag in the middle of the bottom edge. Sew as far as the end of the outer fabric, then repeat on the other side. Sew up the lining in the same way, but leaving a turning opening of about 8cm (3¼in) along the bottom, and make sure that you do not accidentally sew the flap as well. Turn the back right side out and sew up the turning opening.

10 Mark the middle of the flap and attach the loop about 1cm (½in) above the bottom edge in accordance with the manufacturer's instructions. Thread the elastic cord through the hook and determine how long you want it to be. To make a cover for the end of the cord, fold a 4 x 4cm (1½ x 1½in) piece of wax cloth, felt or similar material in half. Sew the right side edge, thread in the cord, and then neatly sew up the left side edge. Then sew a horizontal seam over the cover, catching the cord in the stitches. Trim the remainder of the fabric.

Materials

- A: red and white fabric (main piece), 50 x 70cm (19¾ x 27½in)
- B: green and white fabric (outer pockets), 70 x 70cm (27½ x 27½in)
- C: blue fabric with white dots (lining), 50 x 70cm (19¾ x 27½in)
- D: medium iron-on volume fleece, 50 x 70cm (19¾ x 27½in)
- 1 magnetic button, 20mm (¾in)
- 1 snap hook, 15mm (⅔in)
- Bias binding in blue with white dots, 18mm (¾in) wide, two pieces 25cm (9¾in) long
- Scraps of interfacing
- Sewing thread in red, light green and blue

Cutting out

Dimensions and patterns include 0.5cm (¼in) seam allowance.
- A: 2 pieces of pattern 5a
- B: 2 pieces of pattern, 5b 1 strip c measuring 16.5 x 4cm (6½ x 1½in)
- C: 2 pieces of pattern 5a
- D: 2 pieces of pattern 5a

Bag Organiser

Size: 16 x 23 x 7.5cm (6¼ x 9 x 3in) • Pattern pieces: 5a–b on pages 57 and 59
Level of difficulty: ♡ ♡ ♡

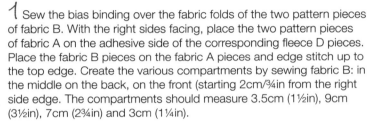

How to do it

1 Sew the bias binding over the fabric folds of the two pattern pieces of fabric B. With the right sides facing, place the two pattern pieces of fabric A on the adhesive side of the corresponding fleece D pieces. Place the fabric B pieces on the fabric A pieces and edge stitch up to the top edge. Create the various compartments by sewing fabric B: in the middle on the back, on the front (starting 2cm/¾in from the right side edge. The compartments should measure 3.5cm (1½in), 9cm (3½in), 7cm (2¾in) and 3cm (1¼in).

2 Attach the magnetic button in accordance with the manufacturer's instructions to fabrics C/5a at 3cm (1¼in) from the top. Iron a remnant of interfacing onto the wrong side of the fabric as reinforcement.

3 For the snap hook attachment, fold strip B/c crosswise with the right sides facing and edge stitch on all sides, leaving a turning opening. Turn right side out. Iron and edge stitch on all sides. Push through the snap hook and fold in half. Place on fabric C/5a (with the ends facing the edge of the fabric) and tack close to the top edge about 3cm (1¼in) from the right side edge, leaving about 0.5cm (¼in) protruding.

4 With the right sides facing, place fabrics C/5a on the front and back of the organiser and edge stitch together, making sure that fabric C and the snap hook are sewn onto the back. Sew the snap hook tape to fabric C about 0.5cm (¼in) from the top edge to reinforce it.

5 Pin the front and back together neatly with the right sides facing. Edge stitch along the bottom of the organiser. Sew up the sides as far as the lining. Sew the bottom corners together, aligning the side seam to the seam at the bottom, and sew up the opening. Sew up the lining in the same way, leaving a turning opening of about 10cm (4in) at the bottom.

6 Turn the organiser right side out, and neaten the corners. Fold the seam allowance of the turning opening to the inside and machine sew the opening. Then edge stitch all around the top edge.

Materials

- A: owl patterned fabric (outer pocket)
  20 x 140cm (7¾ x 55in)
- B: green polka dot patterned fabric (front/
  back of bag) 20 x 30cm (7¾ x 11¾in)
- C: green fabric (lighting) 35 x 12cm
  (13¾ x 4¾in)
- D: medium iron-on volume fleece,
  35 x 12cm (13¾ x 4¾in)
- light blue piping with white dots,
  22cm (8¾in)
- light blue bias binding with white dots,
  5cm (2in) in length and 2cm (¾in) wide
- light blue bias binding with white dots
  15cm (6in) in length and 2cm (¾in) wide
- 1 button to cover, 1.5m–2cm (⅔–¾in)
  diameter
- 1 metal grommet, 5mm (¼in) diameter
- 1 snap hook with ring attachment,
  2.5 x 4cm (1 x 1½in)
- 1 stud, 9mm (⅓in) diameter
- sewing thread in light blue and green
- pins

Cutting out

Dimensions include 0.5cm (¼in) seam
allowance.

- A: 1 rectangle a of 18 x 9.2cm
  (7 x 3 ⅔in), 1 strip b of 6 x 92cm (2½ x
  36¼in) for the waist strap
- B: 2 rectangles c of 14.5 x 9.2cm
  (5¾ x 3 ⅔in)
- C and D: on completion of the bag
  (see instructions for step 6)

Phone Bag

Size: 13 x 8cm (5 x 3¼in) • Level of difficulty: ♡ ♡ ♡

How to do it

1 To make the button loop, fold the 15cm (6in) piece of bias binding in half lengthwise. Fold it so you have a triangle in the middle at the bottom, leaving the raw edges on the outside. Pin and edge stitch the bias binding along the outer edges.

2 Fold the 5cm (2in) piece of bias binding in half to 2.5cm (1in), then edge stitch and fit the metal grommet 0.7cm (¼in) from the folded edge. Cover the button in fabric A in accordance with the manufacturer's instructions.

3 For the waist strap, fold the short edges of strip A/b over by about 1cm (½in) and place together at an angle with the right sides facing. Pin. Edge stitch all round, leaving a turning opening (the strap must be exactly 2.5cm (1in) wide later on in order to fit through the snap hook). Turn right side out, iron and edge stitch.

4 Fold fabric A/a in half crosswise (to 9 x 9.2cm/3½ x 3⅔in), iron and sew the piping to the inside of the folded edge. Place the outer bag with the raw edges flush on the right side of the front (B) and tack along the bottom edge to secure. Place the back (B) on the front with the right sides facing. Edge stitch all the layers together along the bottom and neaten with zigzag stitch.

5 Turn the items right side out. Edge stitch the bottom of the front to the outside pocket, and pin the outer pocket to the front.

6 For the lining, open out the bag, place on lining (C) and volume fleece (D) and cut to the same size. Fold the lining to about 7 x 9.2cm (2¾ x 3 ⅔in) and cut along the folded edge (= front and back). Iron the opened-out back onto the adhesive side of fleece D.

7 Sew the button loop onto the middle of the bottom edge of the back using zigzag stitch.

8 Place the lining pieces on the front or back, right sides facing, and edge stitch to the top and bottom edges.

9 Fold the front and back together with the right sides facing, making sure that all the seams and transitions are placed together neatly, and pin.

10 Edge stitch on all sides, leaving a turning opening of about 5cm (2in) at the bottom. Turn the bag right side out and neaten the corners. Then fold the lining seam allowances to the inside, and machine sew the opening. Tuck the lining into the bag.

11 Fold the waist strap in half lengthwise. Place one end around the ring of the snap hook and catch the other in between so that the ends overlap by about 3cm (1¼in) and the strap is closed. Pin, then sew at 0.5cm (¼in) and 1cm (⅜in) from the bottom edge. Attach the stud in the middle of the overlap.

12 To sew on the button, use the attached loop to establish the exact position on the front. Put the device in the bag to do this. Sew on the button.

Note

The cover is suitable for a phone measuring a maximum of 11.5 x 6.2 x 1.2cm (4½ x 2⅓ x ½in). Use the following calculation for all other devices:

- Height + depth + 1cm (⅜in) (seam allowance = height on fabric fold)
- Width + depth + 1cm (⅜in) seam allowance = width
- Adjust the height of the outside pocket (A) accordingly; it should be 5cm (2in) shorter than fabric B.

Materials

- ♥ A: patterned white wax cloth (front/back, compartments), 32 x 80cm (12½ x 31½in)
- ♥ B: black cotton fabric (lining), 25 x 40cm (9¾ x 15¾in)
- ♥ C: medium iron-on volume fleece, 25 x 40cm (9¾ x 15¾in)
- ♥ D: firm iron-on interfacing (interlining), 25 x 40cm (9¾ x 15¾in)
- ♥ 1 press stud, 10mm (³/₈ in) diameter
- ♥ bias binding in black with white dots, 2cm (¾in) wide, 23cm (9in) long
- ♥ 1 white zip, 10cm (4in)
- ♥ zigzag tape in black, 22cm (8¾in)
- ♥ sewing thread in white and black
- ♥ carpet knife
- ♥ ruler

Cutting out

Pattern 6a including 0.5cm (¼in) seam allowance, measurements c, e and pattern 6b including 0.5cm (¼in) seam allowance, no seam allowance required for measurement d.

- ♥ Fabric A: 2 pieces each of patterns 6a and 6b, 1 rectangle c measuring 23 x 33cm (9 x 13in) for the cover, 1 rectangle d measuring 13 x 5cm (5 x 2in) for the pen, 1 rectangle e measuring 13 x 33cm (5 x 13in) for the notepad
- ♥ Fabric B: 1 rectangle c measuring 23 x 33cm (9 x 13in)
- ♥ Fabric C: 1 rectangle c measuring 23 x 33cm (9 x 13in)
- ♥ Fabric D: 1 rectangle c measuring 23 x 33cm (9 x 13in)

Notebook Cover

Size: 15.5 x 21.5cm (6 x 8½in) • **Pattern pieces:** 6a–b on page 60
Level of difficulty: ♡ ♡ ♡

How to do it

1 For the tab, sew the zigzag tape onto the right side of one piece of fabric A/6a, working on the rounded edge of the fabric. Place the counterpart A/6a on top with the right sides facing, and sew together up to the top edge. Turn the tab right side out, iron and edge stitch all round.

2 For the pen holder, fold the top edge of fabric A/d over 0.5cm (¼in) and sew along the folded edge, working very closely to the fold. Place the wrong side on the right side of fabric A/c about 6.5cm (⁵/₈in) above the bottom edge and 5cm (2in) from the right side edge, and sew two parallel seams close to the side and bottom edges.

3 For the cover, iron the wrong side of fabric B onto the right side of interfacing D. Place fleece C neatly beneath it with the wrong sides facing, and zigzag all around the layers to join.

4 For the pad slot, fold the top edge of fabric A/d over by about 0.5cm (¼in) and sew. Place on the lining with the right and bottom edges neatly aligned, and sew into place. Leave the top open.

5 For the two credit card slots, use the carpet knife to cut the slot lines as shown in the pattern on fabric A/6b.

Note

Some wax cloths can only be sewn with a sewing machine foot for Teflon. Alternatively, you can also stick some masking tape around the sewing foot. It's a good idea to find out before you buy the fabric.

6 For the money compartment, use the carpet knife to cut a rectangle from fabric A measuring 1 x 9.5cm (½ x 3¾in) as shown on the pattern. Position the zip in the centre behind the slot, and sew on securely on the right side using the zip foot.

7 Now put the wrong side of this piece A/6b on the right side of the second fabric A/6b and edge stitch all round. Put a credit card in each of the compartments, and edge stitch around the outlines for each compartment. If you want to put several cards in a compartment, make the border a little wider. Sew the bias binding onto the still unfinished right side edge of the compartment.

8 Sew the interior compartment flush left to the lining as far as the bias bound side edge.

9 Shorten the tab to 7.5cm (3in), allowing the unfinished end to protrude 1cm (½in) beyond the side edge, and with the right sides facing tack to the middle of the left side edge of fabric A/c.

10 With the right sides facing, sew the outside of A/c including the tab to the lining, including the inner compartment and notepad opening, leaving a turning opening of about 10cm (4in) at the bottom. Trim the corner seam allowances at an angle. Turn the cover right side out, and carefully neaten the corners.

11 Fold the seam allowances of the turning opened to the inside and secure with a clothes peg or similar item (pins would leave holes in the fabric). Then edge stitch all around the cover, including the turning opening.

12 Insert one half of the press stud into the closing tab, a little distance from the rounded bottom edge, in accordance with the manufacturer's instructions. Put a notepad in the cover. Place the tab around it and mark the point where the other piece of the press stud needs to be attached, and insert it in place.

Tip

The last step is a little tricky. To make it easier, mark the position of the second half on the fabric, and push the pointed side from the outside to the inside. Now take a second pointed side and push it through the point where you can see the zigzags of the first piece shining through. Then put on the counterpiece and push the press stud into place. Take care not to damage the inner compartment.

Materials

- A: patterned fabric in blue (front/back), 50 x 60cm (19¾ x 23½in)
- B: patterned fabric in light green (compartments), 25 x 40cm (9¾ x 15¾in)
- C: plain fabric in blue (lining), 35 x 20cm (13¾ x 7¾in)
- D: turquoise fabric with white dots (lining zip compartment), 25 x 20cm (9¾ x 7¾in)
- E: medium iron-on volume fleece, 35 x 20cm (13¾ x 7¾in)
- F: firm iron-on interfacing (interlining), 25 x 30cm (9¾ x 11¾in)
- 1 zip in blue, 15cm (6in)
- bias binding in turquoise with white dots, 18mm (¾in wide), 16cm (6¼in)
- sewing thread in petrol and lemon
- 1 twist purse closure, 3.5 x 2cm (1⅓ x ¾in)
- carpet knife or scissors

Cutting out

Dimensions include 0.5cm (¼in) seam allowance.

- A: 1 rectangle a of 30.6 x 16.5cm (12 x 6½in), 3 rectangles b of 22 x 16.5cm (8¾ x 6½in)
- B: 2 rectangles b of 22 x 16.5cm (8¾ x 6½in)
- C: 1 rectangle a of 30.6 x 16.5cm (12 x 6½in)
- D: 1 rectangle b of 22 x 16.5cm (8¾ x 6½in)
- E: 1 rectangle a of 30.6 x 16.5cm (12 x 6½in)
- F: 1 rectangle a of 30.6 x 16.5 cm (12 x 6½in)

Purse

Size: 12 x 15cm (4¾ x 6in) • **Level of difficulty:** ♡ ♡ ♡

How to do it

1 For the card compartments, fold two fabrics of A/b and two fabrics of B in half and edge stitch. Place one fabric B on the table, and put one fabric A/a on top 0.7cm (⅔in) from the top edge. Place a credit card between the two layers. Mark the bottom edge of the card with a pin, and sew the fabric layers together about 2mm (⅛in) towards the right edge. Then sew together the fabrics B and A/b in the same way. Fold the bias binding in half and hold against the last seam. Determine where to cut the bottom edges so that the end seam is just covered. Shorten (cut) the bottom edges accordingly.

2 Next, sew the middle seam from the bottom to the top. Put a credit card in the top compartment and run a fingernail down its edge. Align the mark with the left edge of the sewing foot, and sew the seam with the needle in the middle. Sew the seam three times along the top edge of the compartment openings. Sew the left credit card section in the same way. Sew the bias binding to the bottom edge of the compartments. Set aside.

3 For the zip compartment, with the right sides facing sew the zip flush against the top edge of the remaining fabric A/b (so the underside of the zip should be on the top and the zip pull on the left). About 1cm (⅜in) of the metal end piece of the zip should be on the fabric. Place fabric D/b on fabric A/b neatly and with the right sides facing, and pin the zip. Sew the top edges together with the zip foot, then open out and iron. Edge stitch the edge just below the zip.

4 Now place the bottom edge of fabric A/b flush against the other side of the zip with the right sides facing. Pin and then sew together fabric D with the outer fabric and zip. Open the zip all the way. Turn the items right side out, pull tight, and sew the second edge (this is a little fiddly). Press the bag flat with the zip aligned about 2cm (¾in) below the top edge, and iron.

5 Now sew on the various parts of the interior, ironing fabric C to the adhesive side of fleece E. Place the zip compartment flush against the bottom edge of fabric C and edge stitch together. Sew a second, offset seam along the top edge.

6 Place the credit card compartment on the lining 1.5cm (½in) above the zip compartment, secure, and sew onto the bias binding. Iron interfacing F onto the wrong side of fabric A/a. With the right sides facing, place fabric A/a neatly onto the interior of the purse and sew all round, leaving a turning opening of about 10cm (4in) along the bottom. Trim the corner seam allowances at an angle and carefully turn the purse right side out. Iron. Turn the seam allowance of the turning opening to the inside and pin. Edge stitch the flap and the bottom edge of the purse to close the turning opening.

7 To attach the purse closure, mark the middle of the flap 1.7cm (½in) from the top. Put the locking part for the flap in the middle, and draw on the curve. Use scissors to cut the fabric within the round without getting too close to the drawn edge. Attach the closure in accordance with the manufacturer's instructions, and neaten the area around the curve. This is a little tricky to do, and is easiest done with scissors or a carpet knife.

8 Position the bottom part of the closure (the turning part) on the folded piece of the purse so that it is easy to close. Push the sharp points lightly onto the fabric, and cut the indentations with a carpet knife. Be sure to open the change compartment first and insert something as protection to prevent damage to the other fabric pieces. Now pierce the sharp points through the fabric and push to the outside.

Pencil Case

Size: 5 x 18.5cm (2 x 7¼in) • **Pattern piece:** 7 on page 60

Level of difficulty: ♡

Materials

- A: snail patterned fabric (front/back), 20 x 27cm (7¾ x 10¾in)
- B: red fabric with white dots (lining), 20 x 27cm (7¾ x 10¾in)
- C: thick, fluffy volume fleece, 20 x 27cm (7¾ x 10¾in)
- 1 red zip, 20cm (7¾in)
- satin ribbon, 20cm (7¾in)
- 2 wooden beads in red and pink
- sewing thread in white and red

Cutting out

Pattern includes 0.5cm (¼in) seam allowance.
- A: 1 piece of pattern 7
- B: 1 pieces of pattern 7
- C: 1 piece of pattern 7

How to do it

1 For the outside, place fabric A on fleece C and sew the top and bottom edges together using zigzag stitch. With the right sides facing, sew the zip flush against the top edge of fabric A (the underside of the zip should be on the top and the zip pull on the left).

2 For the lining, fold fabric B along the fabric fold and cut open (= front and back). With the right sides facing, put fabric B on fabric A and pin the zip with the top edges flush against each other. Using the zipper foot, sew along the top edges.

3 Open out the fabrics and, with the right sides facing, pin the free side of the zip flush to the opposite top edge of fabric A. Sew the remaining fabric B to the zip and the top edge of fabric A. The right side of the lining will be on the inside.

4 With the right sides facing, neatly sew the side edges of the case together. Sew the bottom corners together, aligning the side seam to the seam at the bottom, and sew up the opening.

5 Sew the side and bottom seams of the lining together in the same way, leaving a turning opening of about 7cm (2¾in) at the bottom. Turn the bag right side out. Carefully shape the corners of the outer fabric and lining. Fold the seam allowance of the turning opening to the inside, and sew up on the machine. Tuck the lining to the inside.

6 Thread the satin ribbon through the hole in the zip pull. Grasp the two ends of the ribbon and thread them through the wooden beads. Knot to secure.

Materials

- ♥ A: natural linen (front/back),
  25 x 35cm (9¾ x 13¾in)
- ♥ B: patterned natural linen (outer pocket),
  32 x 35cm (12½ x 13¾in)
- ♥ C: white cotton (lining), 45 x 17cm
  (17¾ x 6¾in)
- ♥ D: medium iron-on volume fleece,
  45 x 17cm (17¾ x 6¾in)
- ♥ white piping, 15cm (6in)
- ♥ elastic cord, 2mm (⅛in) diameter,
  15cm (6in)
- ♥ 1 button to cover, 2cm (¾in) diameter
- ♥ sewing threads in white and to match
  the natural linen

Cutting out

Dimensions include 0.5cm (¼in)
seam allowance.

- ♥ A: 2 rectangles of 20.5 x 15cm (8 x 6in)
- ♥ B: 1 rectangle of 30 x 15cm
  (11¾ x 6in)
- ♥ C: 1 piece on completion of the bag
  (see instructions, step 2)
- ♥ D: 1 piece on completion of the bag
  (see instructions, step 2)

Tablet Case

Size: 19 x 14cm (7½ x 5½in) • Level of difficulty: ♡

Sewing

1 To make the outer pocket, fold fabric B in a square with the wrong side facing and iron. Sew the piping onto the inside of the fabric fold. Place the outer bag with the raw edges flush on the right side of the front (A) and tack along the bottom edge to secure. Place the back (A) on the front with the right sides facing. Edge stitch all the layers together along the bottom, and neaten the seam allowance with zigzag stitch.

2 Turn the items right side out. Edge stitch along the bottom edge of the outside pocket and pin to the front. For the lining, open out the bag, place on lining (C) and fleece (D) and cut to the same size. Fold the lining in half across the middle and cut along the fold (front and back). Iron the opened-out back onto the adhesive side of fleece D. Lay the elastic cord in a loop and sew to the middle of the bottom edge using zigzag stitch. There should be approx. 4cm (1½in) of it on the fabric. Place the lining pieces on the top and bottom edges of the bag with the right sides facing, and edge stitch together.

3 Place the front and back together with the right sides facing. Make sure that all the seams are placed together neatly. Sew all around the bag, leaving a turning opening of about 7cm (2¾in) at the bottom.

4 Trim the corner seam allowances at an angle. Turn the bag right side out, and carefully neaten the corners. Fold the seam allowance of the turning opening to the inside. Machine sew the open seam and tuck the lining to the inside.

5 Cover the button in fabric B in accordance with the manufacturer's instructions, and sew on by hand.

Note

The cover is suitable for eReaders measuring a maximum of 17.2 x 12 x 1cm (7 x 4¾ x 3/8in), e.g. Kindle. For all other devices, calculate the dimensions of the bag as follows:

- ♥ height + thickness + 1.5cm (½in)
  seam allowance = height
- ♥ width + thickness + 1cm (3/8in)
  seam allowance = width

Materials

- A: white patterned fabric with black flowers (front/back), 25 x 15cm (9¾ x 6in)
- B: black patterned fabric with white flowers (front/back), 15 x 15cm (6 x 6in)
- C: white patterned fabric with a geometric pattern (lining), 32 x 11cm (12½ x 4¼in)
- D: medium iron-on volume fleece, 32 x 11cm (12½ x 4¼in)
- white elastic cord, 2mm (⅛in) diameter, 10cm (4in)
- 1 red button, 15–18mm (½ – ⅝in) diameter
- red piping, 18cm (7in)
- white sewing thread

Cutting out

Dimensions include 0.5cm (¼in) seam allowance.

- A: 2 rectangles of 10 x 9.5cm (4 x 3¾in)
- B: 1 rectangle of 11.5 x 9.5cm (4½ x 3¾in)
- C: on completion of the bag (see instructions)
- D: on completion of the bag (see instructions)

Phone Cover

Size: 13 x 8cm (5 x 3¼in) • Level of difficulty: ♡

How to do it

1 Sew the piping to the top and bottom edges (9.5cm/3¾in wide) of fabric B. With the right sides facing, place fabrics A on the top and bottom edges of fabric B and sew. Make sure that the sewing seam of the piping is not visible (check the needle/sewing foot position). Open out the fabrics and iron so that the piping is facing down. Edge stitch fabric A at the top of the piping. Put the bag on the lining (C) and volume fleece (D) and cut to the same size. Place the bag on fleece D and iron on.

2 Fold the elastic cord in a loop and sew onto the middle of the bottom edge of the bag with three rows of zigzag stitch. Approximately 3.5–4cm (1⅜–1½in) of the loop will be on the fabric. Fold fabric C in half crossways (to 14 x 9.5cm/5½ x 3¾in) and cut along the fabric fold. Place one piece neatly on the back of the bag with the right sides facing and sew together along the top edge. Repeat for the front.

3 Pin the bag sides together neatly with the right sides facing, making sure that the points where the fabrics cross are exactly together. Sew together all around, leaving a turning opening of about 5cm (2in) at the bottom. Turn the bag right side out. Fold the seam allowance of the lining to the inside, and machine sew the opening. Tuck the lining to the inside. Iron the cover. Place the cord loop on the front and determine the position of the button with the phone in the cover. Sew the button onto the front by hand.

Materials

- A: blue floral patterned fabric (flap), 10 x 17cm (4 x 6¾in)
- B: light blue patterned fabric with white dots (main bag), 20 x 18cm (7¾ x 7in)
- C: dark blue patterned fabric with white dots (lining), 30 x 18cm (11¾ x 7in)
- D: medium iron-on volume fleece, 20 x 18cm (7¾ x 7in)
- E: lightweight iron-on interfacing, 10 x 17cm (4 x 6¾in)
- white piping, 30cm (11¾in)
- 1 fastener, 15 x 22mm (½ x ¾in)
- sewing thread in light and dark blue
- punch pliers

Cutting out

Patterns include 0.5cm (¼in) seam allowance.

- A: 1 piece of pattern 9a
- B: 2 pieces of pattern 9b
- C: 1 piece of pattern 9a, 2 pieces of pattern 9b
- D: 2 pieces of pattern 9b
- E: 1 piece of pattern 9a

Tissue Case

Size: 7 x 15 x 2cm (2¾ x 6 x ¾in) • Pattern pieces: 9a–b on page 62
Level of difficulty: ♡ ♡

How to do it

1 Iron interfacing E onto the back of fabric A. Lay the piping flush with the rounded edge on the right side of fabric A and sew into place. Place fabric C/9a on fabric A with the right sides facing and sew along the outer edge. The top stays open. Turn right side out, iron and edge stitch.

2 Iron fabrics B onto fleece D. Place fabric C/9b on fabric B with the right sides facing and sew along the top edge. With the right sides of the fabric facing, place the flap on the middle of the second fabric B. Place fabric C/9b on top with the right sides facing and edge stitch the layers together along the top edge. Pin the front and back together with the right sides facing. Pin the lining together. Make sure that the seams are all lying neatly on top of each other. Edge stitch along the bottom edge of the bag, then sew up the two side edges to the middle of the bottom edge of the lining, leaving a turning opening of 5cm (2in) in the middle at the bottom.

3 Sew the bottom corners of the lining and bag together, aligning the side seam to the seam at the bottom and sew up the opening. Turn the bag right side out and neaten the corners. Fold the seam allowance of the turning opening to the inside, and sew up the opening. Tuck the lining to the inside and iron.

4 Put the top part of the closure on the middle of the flap and attach in accordance with the manufacturer's instructions. Punch the holes with punch pliers. Establish the position for the bottom part of the closure and attach in accordance with the manufacturer's instructions.

Materials

For one key ring:
- A: strawberry patterned fabric (front/back), 20 x 10cm (7¾ x 4in)
- B: polka dot patterned fabric (lining), 9 x 10cm (3½ x 4in)
- C: medium iron-on volume fleece, 9 x 10cm (3½ x 4in)
- red hook and loop fastening, 1.5cm (½in)
- cotton webbing in pink and red, 4.5cm (1¾in)
- 1 key ring, 3cm (1¼in) diameter
- sewing thread in pink and red

Cutting out

Dimensions include 0.5cm (¼in) seam allowance.
- A: 1 rectangle a of 9 x 7 cm (3½ x 2¾in), 1 rectangle b of 8.5 x 7cm (3¼ x 2¾in)
- B: 1 rectangle b of 8.5 x 9cm (3¼ x 3½in)
- C: 1 rectangle b of 8.5 x 9cm (3¼ x 3½in), 1 rectangle c of 4.5 x 7cm (1¾ x 2¾in)

Fabric Key Ring

Size: 4.5 x 6cm (1¾ x 2½in)

Level of difficulty: ♡

How to do it

1 For the bag, fold fabric A/a in half (to 4.5 x 7cm/1¾ x 2¾in), iron and insert fleece C/c. Position the cotton webbing in a loop and edge stitch securely to just under the top edge on the right side. Sew the item all round to the fabric fold.

2 Place the hook side of the hook and loop fastener on the middle of the fabric 0.5cm (¼in) from the top edge, and sew.

3 Place fabric B/b on fleece C/b, and fabric A/b on top flush with the bottom edge. Place fabric A/a on top with the right sides facing. The piece of the fabric that will later be the flap is facing up.

4 Sew all around the key holder as far as the bottom edge. Trim the corner seam allowances at an angle and turn the key holder right side out. Make sure that both the lining and the back seam of the hook and loop fastener is visible when turned.

5 Carefully shape the corners of the key holder, and smooth the fabric.

6 Sew up the turning opening approximately 0.5cm (¼in) above the bottom edge. Neaten with zigzag stitch and turn right side out. Iron, and place the fleecy part of the hook and loop fastening on the middle of the flap on the inside. Sew 1cm (½in) from the top edge. Pull the key ring through the webbing.

Materials

- ♥ A: light blue fabric with white dots (front and back), 10 x 22cm (4 x 8¾in)
- ♥ B: fabric in a fish pattern (front/back), 12 x 25cm (4¾ x 9¾in)
- ♥ C: light blue fabric (lining), 20 x 25cm (7¾ x 9¾in)
- ♥ D: medium iron-on volume fleece, 12 x 25cm (4¾ x 9¾in)
- ♥ 1 snap hook, 8cm (3¼in)
- ♥ zigzag tape in white, 18cm (7in)
- ♥ green piping with white dots, 18cm (7in)
- ♥ bias binding, 2cm (¾in) wide, green with white dots, 6cm (2½in)
- ♥ link chain with catch (DIY store), 20cm (7¾in)
- ♥ 1 key ring, 1.5cm (½in) diameter
- ♥ 2 metal grommets, 5mm (¼in) diameter
- ♥ sewing thread in light and dark blue
- ♥ punch pliers

Cutting out

Patterns include 0.5cm (¼in) seam allowance.

- ♥ A: 2 pieces of pattern 8a
- ♥ B: 2 pieces of pattern 8b
- ♥ C: 2 pieces on completion of the bag (see instructions, step 3)
- ♥ D: 2 pieces of pattern 8b

Key Case

Size: 12.5 x 8cm (4¾ x 3¼in) • Pattern pieces: 8a–b on page 62
Level of difficulty: ♡ ♡

How to do it

1 For the front and back, iron fabric B wrong side to right on the adhesive side of fleece D. Place the zigzag tape neatly on the top and bottom edges of fabric B and edge stitch.

2 Fold the bias binding in half and edge stitch. Draw through the snap hook, fold in half and sew onto the right side edge about 1.5cm (½in) below the top edge. The loop and snap hook will be about 2.5cm (1in) on the front. Sew the outer edge of the bias binding neatly to fabric B. Check to establish which position the sewing foot and needle need to be in so that only the bottom edge of the zigzag piping will be seen later.

3 For the panel, sew fabric A to fabric B (front/back) with the right sides facing, then sew and iron. Place the finished front and back on fabric C (lining) and cut out twice.

4 Measure 5cm (2in) from the top edge of the front and back pieces (outside/lining) and mark with pins. With the right sides facing, sew the two front pieces (outside/lining) to the top edge. Repeat for the two back pieces.

5 Open out the two pieces. Pin together with the right sides facing, making sure that the markings are exactly together. Sew up the side and bottom edges from marking to marking, but leave a turning opening of about 5cm (2in) at the bottom of the lining.

6 In order to sew up the 5cm (2in) side edges, open out the fabrics so that the seams between the fabric of the case and fabric C are together.

7 Sew the side edges completely, but only as far as the existing side seam (do not sew over the seam).

8 Turn the case right side out and carefully work the fabric from the inside out. Fold the seam allowances of the turning opening to the inside. Machine sew the open seam and tuck the lining to the inside.

9 Iron the top edge of the case well and tuck to the inside so that the snap hook can easily be pushed through the resulting tube (don't forget the seam allowance!). Pin the fabric and edge stitch along the bottom edge with the zip foot (the needle is on the left side).

10 Repeat for the back, making sure that the back and front are at the same height. In accordance with the manufacturer's instructions, mark the holes for the metal grommets on the back of the case as shown on pattern piece 8b. It's easy with punch pliers, but do make sure that you do not also punch a hole through the front of the fabric as well. Fit the metal grommets and thread the link chain through them from the inside. Insert the key ring on the inside and secure.

11 Push the two parts of the snap hook through the respective tubes, and secure on the other side in accordance with the manufacturer's instructions.

Tablet Cover

Size: 25 x 20.5cm (9¾ x 8in) • Level of difficulty: ♡ ♡ ♡

Materials

- A: patterned fabric with coloured dots (front and back, interior compartment), 29 x 65cm (11½ x 25½in)
- B: bird patterned fabric (strap, interior compartment, corners), 36 x 35cm (14¼ x 13¾in)
- C: green fabric with white dots (lining), 29 x 45cm (11½ x 17¾in)
- D: medium iron-on volume fleece, 29 x 45cm (11½ x 17¾in)
- bias binding in pink with white dots, 2cm (¾in wide), 27cm (10¾in)
- 1 plastic buckle in green, 30mm (1¼in)
- sewing thread in white and pink

Cutting out

Dimensions include 0.5cm (¼in) seam allowance.

- A: 1 rectangle c of 26.5 x 43cm (10½ x 17in), 1 rectangle d of 26.5 x 36cm (10½ x 14¼in)
- B: 2 squares a of 6.5 x 6.5cm (2½ x 2½in), 2 squares b of 7 x 7cm (2¾ x 2¾in), 2 strips f of 18 x 6.4cm (7 x 25/8in), 1 rectangle e of 33 x 18cm (13 x 7in)
- C: 1 rectangle measuring 26.5 x 43cm (10½ x 17in)
- D: 1 rectangle measuring 26.5 x 43cm (10½ x 17in)

Sewing

1 For the triangular corners (to hold the tablet), fold squares B/a diagonally with the wrong sides facing and iron. Place the two corners B/b together with the right sides facing, and edge stitch along one side. Turn right side out and iron.

2 For the interior compartments, fold rectangle B/e in half across the middle with the wrong sides facing (to 16.5 x 18cm/6½ x 7in) and iron. Fold rectangle A/d in half across the middle with the wrong sides facing (to 26.5 x 18cm/10½ x 7in) and iron.

3 Place part B/e on part A/d and edge stitch along the bottom edge.

4 Attach the bias binding to the 26.5cm (10½in) folded edge.

5 For the lining, iron the wrong side of fabric part C to the adhesive side of fleece D. Align the interior compartments on the right fabric side of part C along the left (26.5cm/10½in) side edge, then pin and sew along the top and bottom edges.

6 Sew the corners to the right fabric side and the right half of the lining, sewing the triangles of B/a to the right top and side edge and the right bottom and side edge. Place the triangles of B/b on the top and bottom edges with the sewn corners facing left. The raw fabric edges will align with the bottom and top edges respectively. The seam edges of the triangles of B/b should be 21.5cm (8½in) from the right side edge. Pin the corners, and edge stitch along the side, top and bottom edges. Sew the exposed edges three times.

7 For the strap, fold strips B/f in half lengthwise with the right sides facing (to 3cm/1¼ inches wide) and sew together all round apart from one short side. Turn right side out and carefully shape the corners. Iron and edge stitch all round.

8 Place rectangle A/c with the right side facing up. Edge stitch the two straps to the top and bottom edges 4.5cm (1¾in) from the left side edge. Then place rectangle A/c on the lining with the right sides facing. The straps will now be on the right side. Pin the layers together neatly and sew all round, leaving a turning opening of approximately 10cm (4in) on the right side edge.

9 Trim the corner seam allowances at an angle. Turn the cover right side out, and carefully neaten the corners then iron. Fold the seam allowances of the turning opening to the inside and pin the opening.

10 Sew the cover 2mm (⅛in) from the edges, which will also close the turning opening.

11 Feed the upper part of the belt through the top part of the buckle (from back to front, then back again). Feed the bottom part of the belt from the front through the bottom part of the buckle. Fold about 3cm (1¼in) on the back and sew.

Materials

- A: red patterned fabric with white dots (front/back), 20 x 55cm (7¾ x 21¾in)
- B: strawberry patterned fabric (flap), 12 x 25cm (4¾ x 9¾in)
- C: pink patterned fabric with pale pink dots (lining), 20 x 75cm (7¾ x 29½in)
- D: thick, fluffy volume fleece, 20 x 55cm (7¾ x 21¾in)
- E: lightweight iron-on interfacing, 12 x 25cm (4¾ x 9¾in)
- 1 press stud, 10mm (½in) diameter
- bias binding, 18mm (¾in) wide, 15cm (6in)
- 1 button to cover, 15–19mm (½ – ¾in) diameter
- zigzag tape in white, 50cm (19¾in)
- sewing thread in pink and red
- pins

Cutting out

Patterns include 0.5cm (½in) seam allowance.

- A: 2 pieces of pattern 3a
- B: 1 piece of pattern 3b
- C: 2 pieces of pattern 3a, 1 piece of pattern 3b
- D: 2 pieces of pattern 3a
- E: 1 piece of pattern 3b

Make-up Bag

Size: 10.5 x 19cm (4 x 7½in) • **Pattern pieces:** 3a–b on pages 58 and 61
Level of difficulty: ♡ ♡ ♡

How to do it

1 Cover the button in fabric in accordance with the manufacturer's instructions. For the flap, iron interfacing E onto the wrong side of fabric B. Place the outer edge of the zigzag tape neatly on the bottom of fabric B and edge stitch securely. Set the sewing foot and needle position so that only the lower part of the tape is visible after sewing.

2 Place fabric C/3b on fabric B with the right sides facing, and sew together as far as the top edge. Turn right side out, iron and edge stitch.

3 To make the button loop, fold the bias banding in half lengthwise. The raw edges should be on the outside and the tape forms a triangle at the bottom in the middle. Pin, then fit the binding along the outer edges.

4 For the bag, place fabric A on fleece D and sew along the top edge in zigzag stitch. Place fabric C on A (the front), right sides facing, and edge stitch along the top, working close to the edge. Open out the fabrics and edge stitch along the top of the front.

5 With the rights sides of the fabric facing, sew the button loop to the middle of the back. 4–4.5cm (1½–1¾in) of it should be on the fabric with the open edges at the top.

6 With the right sides of the fabric facing, pin the flap to the middle of the top of the back. Then place fabric C on the two other layers with the right side facing and sew. Open out the fabrics and edge stitch along the top of the back.

7 Pin the front and back together with the right sides facing, making sure the seams are neatly aligned. Edge stitch along the bottom.

8 Sew up the sides as far as the lining. Sew the bottom corners together, aligning the side seam to the seam at the bottom, and sew up the opening. Sew the lining in the same way, but leave a turning opening of about 10cm (4in) at the bottom.

9 Turn the make-up bag right side out and neaten the corners. Fold the seam allowances of the turning opening to the inside. Machine sew the open seam and tuck the lining to the inside.

10 Sew on the button. Find the exact centre of the width of the front, and mark it with a pin. Fold the closure onto the front. Determine the exact position of the button, and sew it on. Position the press stud in the middle of the flap, about 0.5cm (¼in) above the bottom edge, and about 5cm (2in) below the top edge.

Materials

- A: fabric in a fox pattern (front/back, flap), 35 x 15cm (13¾ x 6in)
- B: red fabric with white dots (lining, front/back, flap), 35 x 15cm (13¾ x 6in)
- C: medium iron-on volume fleece, 35 x 15cm (13¾ x 6in)
- 1 metal cigarette case, 7 x 10cm (2¾ x 4in)
- textile adhesive
- sewing thread in light blue and red
- pins

Cutting out

Patterns include 0.5cm (½in) seam allowance.

- A: 1 each of patterns 2a and 2b
- B: 1 each of patterns 2a and 2b
- C: 1 each of patterns 2a and 2b

Card Carrier

Size: 10 x 7cm (4 x 2¾in) • Pattern pieces: 2a–b on page 56
Level of difficulty: ♡ ♡

How to do it

1 Iron the wrong side of fabric A/2b to the adhesive side of volume fleece C/2b. Place fabrics B/2b and A/2b together with the right sides facing and sew all round apart from the top edge, with a seam allowance of 0.5cm (¼in). Fold the flap right side out. Work out the corner, then iron and edge stitch along the seams.

2 Iron the wrong side of fabric A/2a to the adhesive side of fleece C/2a. Fold fabric B/2a in half across the middle and cut along the fold (front and back).

3 Place fabrics B/2a and A/2a together with the right sides facing, and sew from left to right along the top edge between the marks (*). Cut across the edges on the inside at an angle to just before the seam, cutting as far as possible into the corners. Take care not to damage the seams.

4 With the right sides facing, align the flap on the middle of the top of the back on fabric A/2a. Place fabric B/2a (back) on it with the right sides facing, and sew the fabric pieces together 0.5cm (¼in) from the edge. Open out the fabric pieces so the lining and flap are on the right. Edge stitch fabric A, which is on the left, along the top edge.

5 Now sew up the sides of the case with a seam allowance of 0.5cm (¼in). Start by pinning the sides together neatly; you might find this a little fiddly to do!

Note

Make sure that the seam allowance is such that the frame fits.

6 Be careful not to sew over the transitions between the outer fabric and the lining. Sew up the corners, placing the side seam on the middle of the bottom piece of fabric. Repeat for the lining, leaving a turning opening of about 5cm (2in) at the bottom. Turn right side out. Carefully shape the corners and iron the top section well. Fold the seam allowance of the turning opening to the inside. Machine sew the open seam and tuck the lining inside.

7 Put the metal frame in the case. Place drops of the textile adhesive on the frame, and push the bottom edge of the flap into it (use a fork, if that makes it easier). Leave the adhesive to dry for 24 hours.

Templates

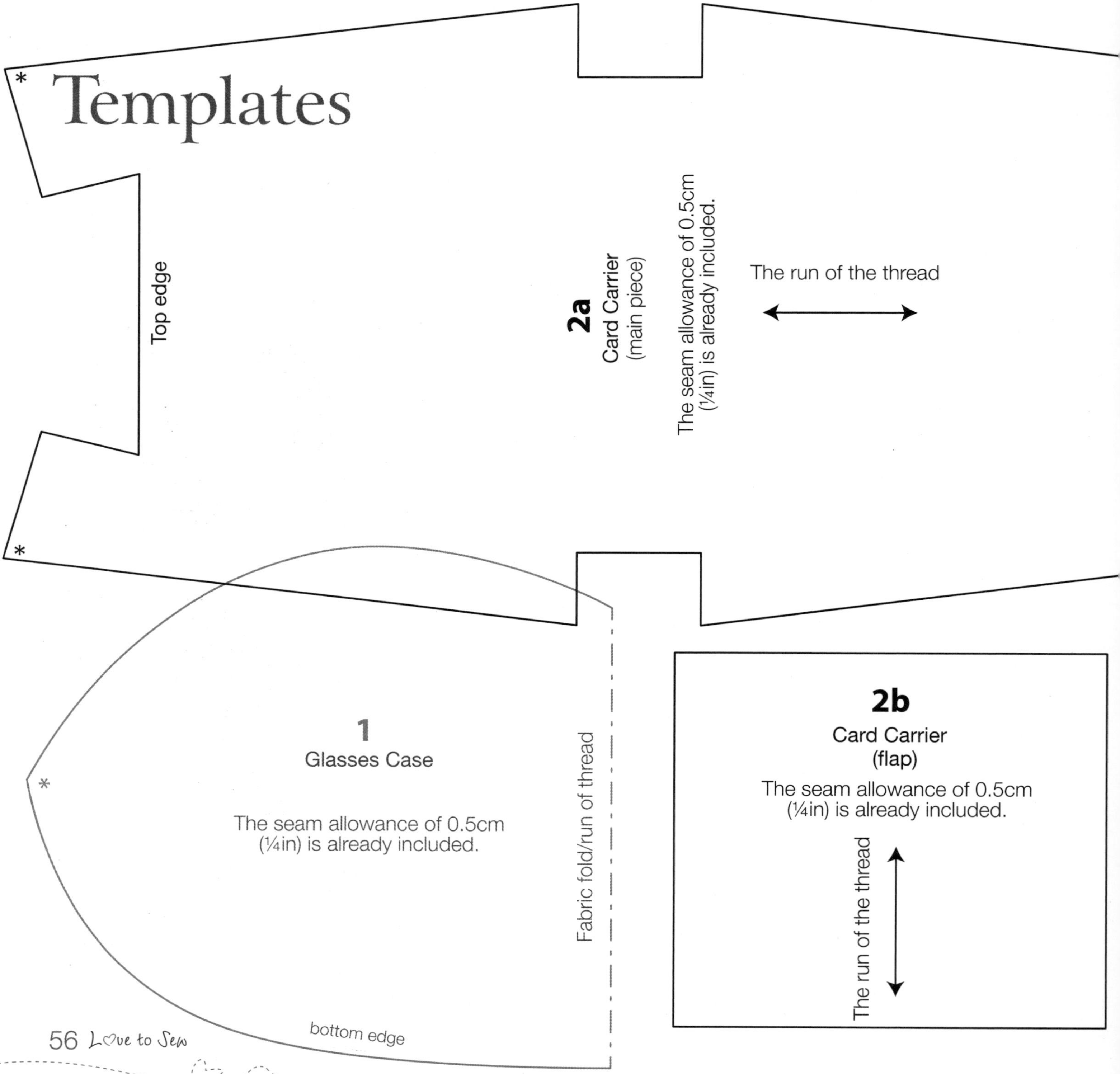

*

Top edge

*

2a
Card Carrier
(main piece)

The seam allowance of 0.5cm
(¼in) is already included.

The run of the thread

←——→

1
Glasses Case

The seam allowance of 0.5cm
(¼in) is already included.

*

Fabric fold/run of thread

bottom edge

2b
Card Carrier
(flap)

The seam allowance of 0.5cm
(¼in) is already included.

The run of the thread

5a

Bag Organiser
(main piece)

The seam allowance of 0.5cm
(¼in) is already included.

Fabric fold/run of thread

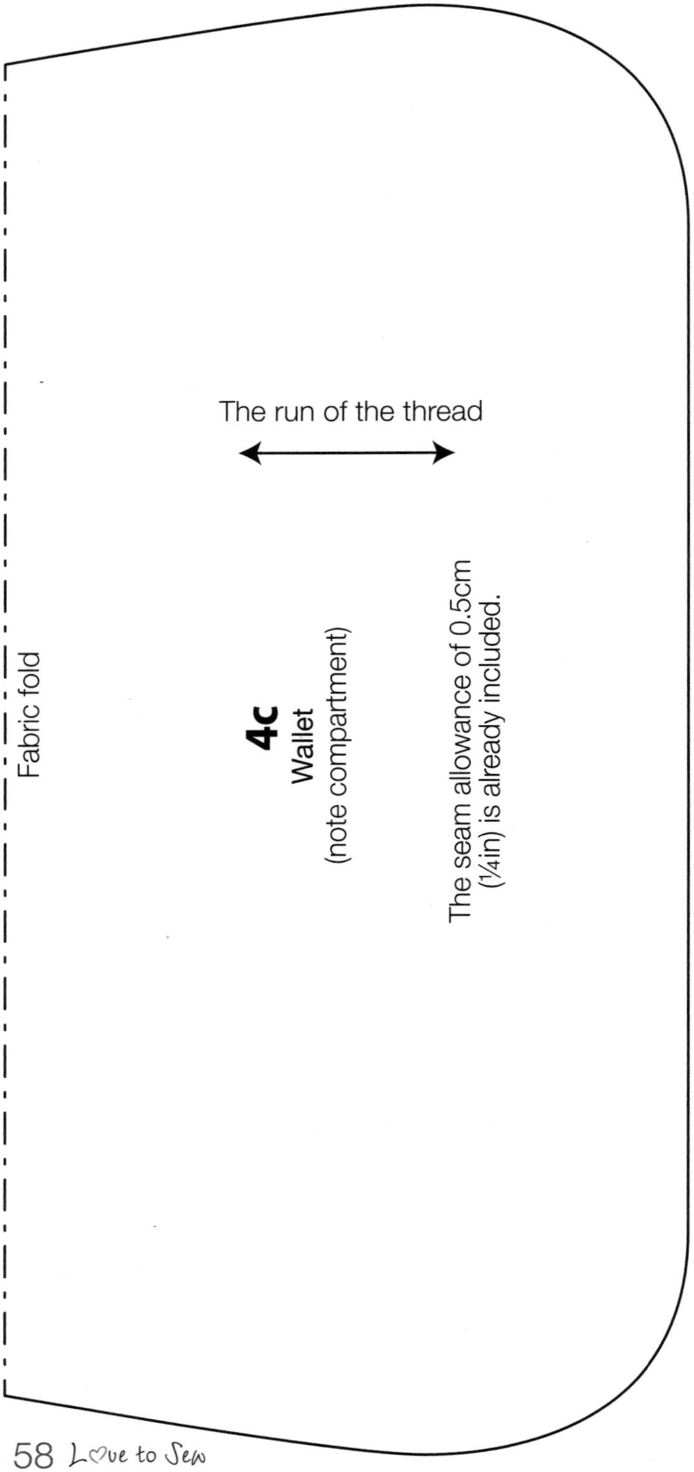

The run of the thread

4c
Wallet
(note compartment)

The seam allowance of 0.5cm
(¼in) is already included.

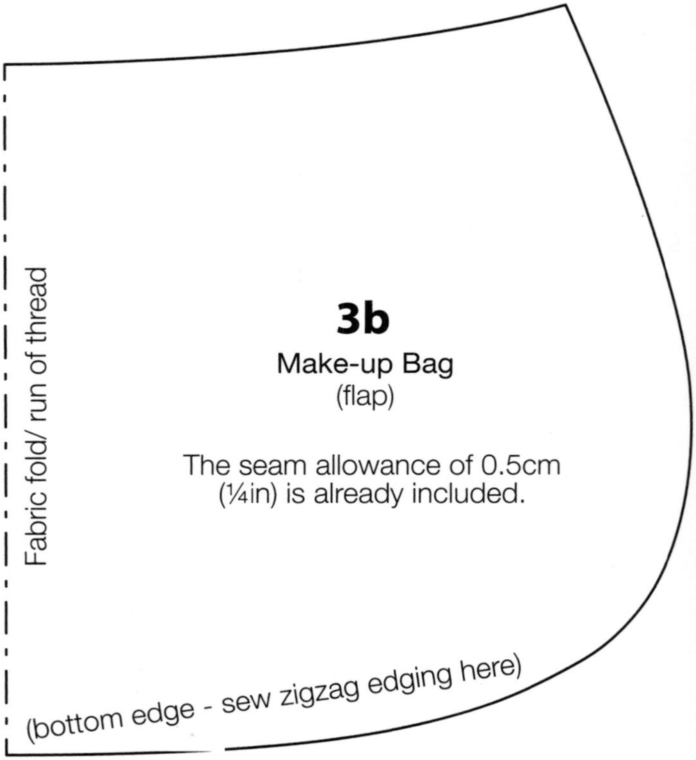

Fabric fold

3b
Make-up Bag
(flap)

The seam allowance of 0.5cm
(¼in) is already included.

Fabric fold/ run of thread

(bottom edge - sew zigzag edging here)

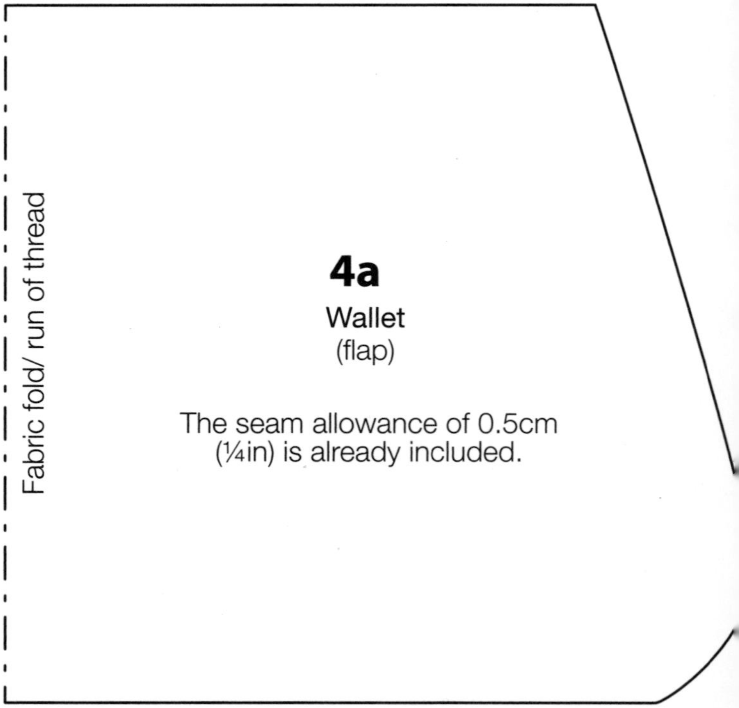

4a
Wallet
(flap)

The seam allowance of 0.5cm
(¼in) is already included.

Fabric fold/ run of thread

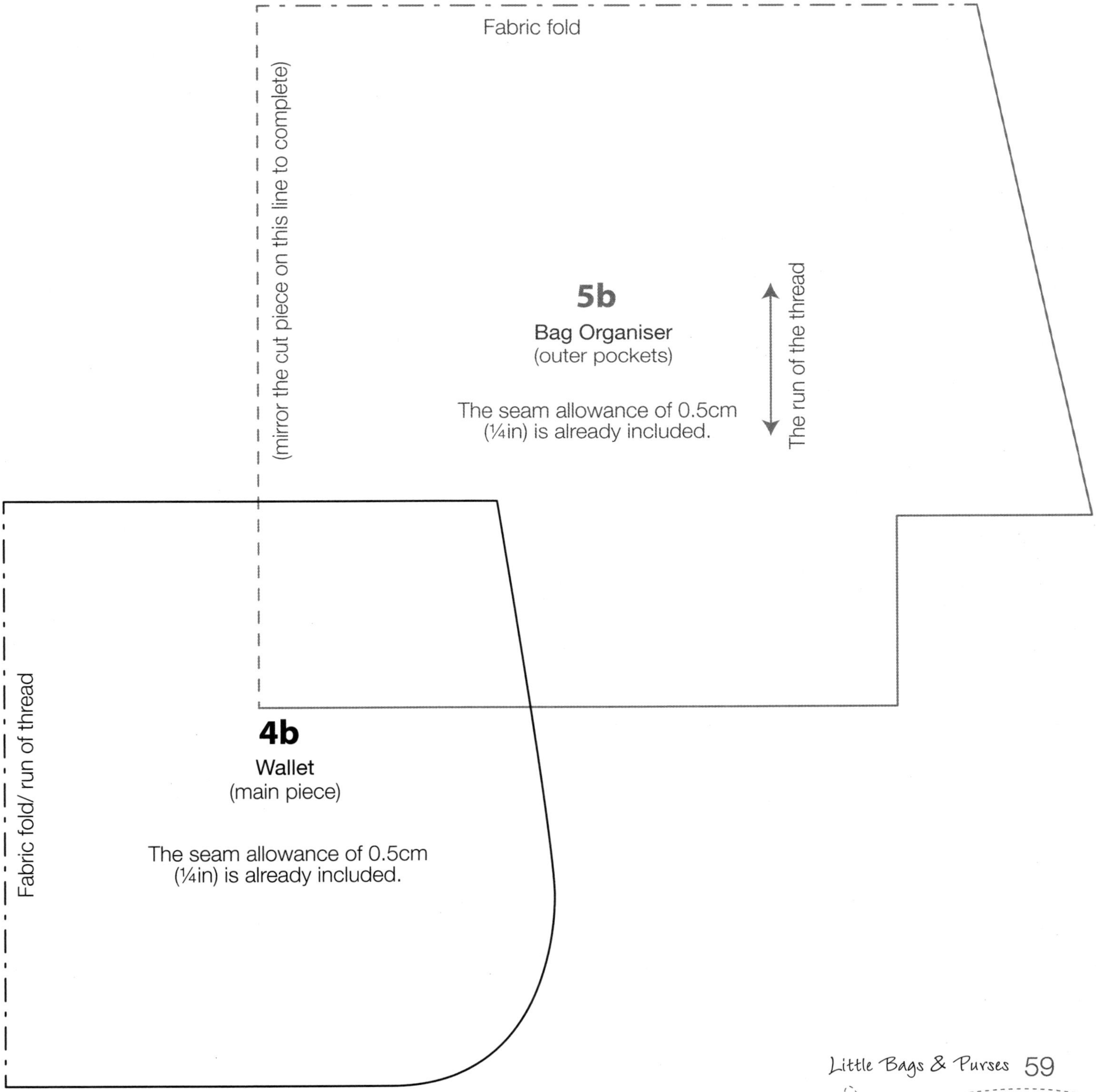

Fabric fold

(mirror the cut piece on this line to complete)

5b

Bag Organiser
(outer pockets)

The seam allowance of 0.5cm
(¼in) is already included.

The run of the thread

4b

Wallet
(main piece)

The seam allowance of 0.5cm
(¼in) is already included.

Fabric fold/ run of thread

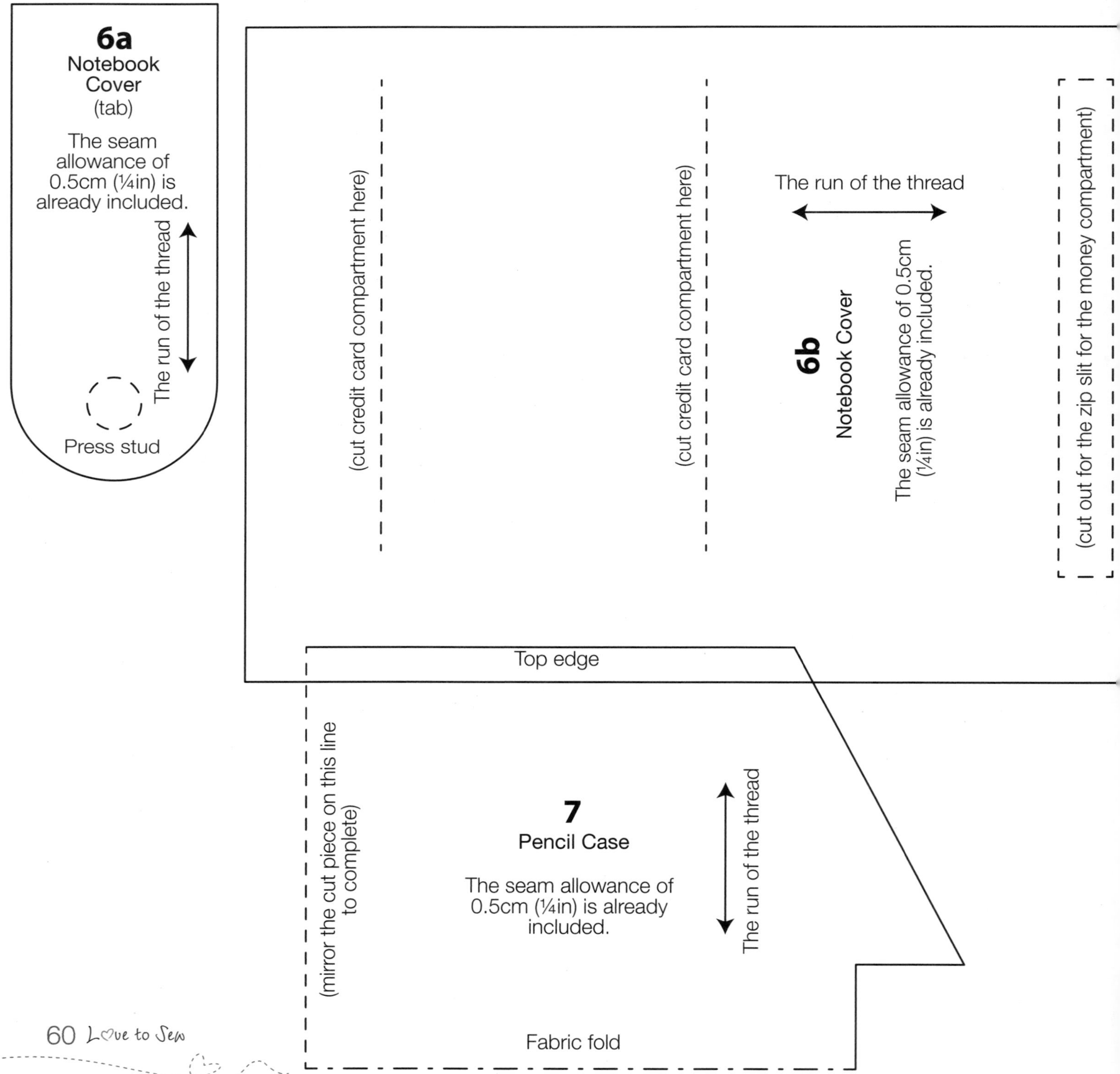

6a

Notebook
Cover
(tab)

The seam
allowance of
0.5cm (¼in) is
already included.

The run of the thread

Press stud

(cut credit card compartment here)

(cut credit card compartment here)

The run of the thread

6b

Notebook Cover

The seam allowance of 0.5cm (¼in) is already included.

(cut out for the zip slit for the money compartment)

Top edge

(mirror the cut piece on this line to complete)

7

Pencil Case

The seam allowance of 0.5cm (¼in) is already included.

The run of the thread

Fabric fold

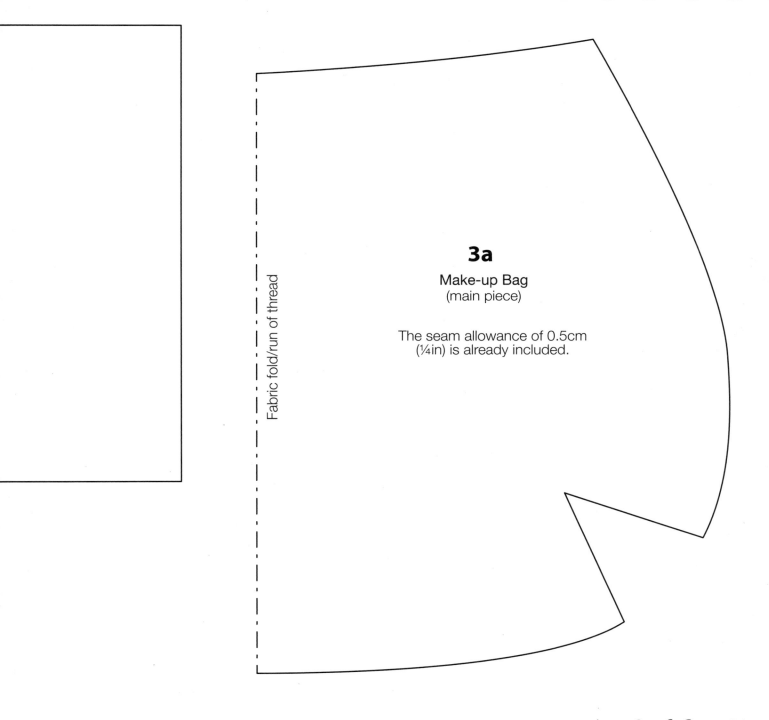

3a

Make-up Bag
(main piece)

The seam allowance of 0.5cm
(¼in) is already included.

Fabric fold/run of thread

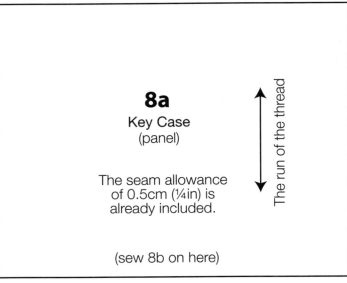

8a

Key Case

(panel)

The seam allowance of 0.5cm (¼in) is already included.

The run of the thread

(sew 8b on here)

9a

Tissue Case

(flap)

The seam allowance of 0.5cm (¼in) is already included.

Fabric fold/ run of thread

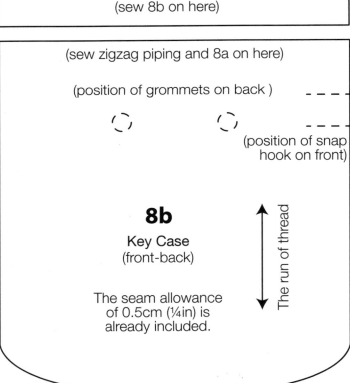

(sew zigzag piping and 8a on here)

(position of grommets on back)

(position of snap hook on front)

8b

Key Case

(front-back)

The run of thread

The seam allowance of 0.5cm (¼in) is already included.

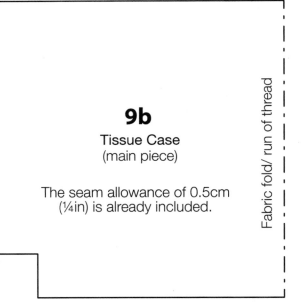

9b

Tissue Case

(main piece)

The seam allowance of 0.5cm (¼in) is already included.

Fabric fold/ run of thread